100 WAYS

TO SAY

NO

100 WAYS TO SAY NO

A People Pleaser's Guide to Setting Boundaries

HOW TO
STOP SAYING YES
WHEN YOU MEAN NO

NICOLE MONENTE

SPRUCE BOOKS
A Sasquatch Books Imprint

For my dad,
who's up there watching
over me, and probably laughing.
I miss that laugh every day.

CONTENTS

FINDING
YOUR NO
MUSCLE

People pleasers have a hard time saying no. There are so many considerations seemingly standing in our way—social pressures and internal pressures, empathy and sympathy, attraction and temptation—not to mention power dynamics. Perceived obligations and actual obligations, presumed consequences and actual consequences . . . oh, and what about guilt?

Sometimes we're even lucky enough to experience them all at once!

Saying yes all the time is not the answer either.

People pleasers will do almost anything to avoid conflict, but at what cost?

A CAUTIONARY TALE
THE STORY OF A GIRL, TURNED PRETZEL, WHO BENT TO THE WILL OF ONE TOO MANY PEOPLE

Learning to set boundaries—and making them stick—is hard.

The truth is, it takes some serious training. The first step is to find your no muscle. It might be a little weak at first.

You don't have to be harsh. Start your training by leaning into the things that come most naturally to you.

People pleasers tend to be empathetic and kind—use those qualities to support your no.

If you can see others' points of view, you're likelier to be able to come up with an authentic way to say no.

The more comfortable you become with saying it, the stronger your no muscle will get—strong enough to be tough when the circumstances call for it.

Feelings—even uncomfortable ones—always pass. So, separate the guilt from the ask. If you don't feel good about the ask, don't let guilt sway you into doing something you don't want to.

If someone mistakes your boundaries as rudeness, remember, that's on them. A healthy relationship cannot be seriously harmed by a polite assertion of boundaries.

Be warned: avoiding conflict in the short term often leads to feelings of resentment in the long term. And, if fear of missing out is driving your aversion to no, keep in mind that there will almost always be a next time—maybe even one you'll want to say yes to.

At the end of the day, you are in control of your life, not some expectation that may or may not be in your head. Reframe all the *shoulds* as *coulds* and go from there!

Sometimes, worrying about the conversation is worse than actually having the conversation.

THE ACTUAL CONVERSATION...

It doesn't always go smoothly, though, especially when egos get in the way.

There are times when you're inevitably going to have to disappoint someone you love. You may not even know where to begin . . .

But if you can get in front of it, so you don't actually have to say anything negative—you can reframe it as a positive.

Turns out the ones you're closest with can have an especially hard time accepting your boundaries.

They've been steering the ship for so long that it may be difficult for them to let you take the wheel.

You need a plan. A good place to start is by appreciating your family's input. Then you can ask them to respect yours.

Validate their concerns and share a bit of your thinking before you hit 'em with the no.

For those *really* tough conversations, you may want to prepare your argument in advance.

Difficult feelings can linger after a hard no.
You might need to just live with them for a while.

Once enough time passes and emotions aren't quite as high, it's worth addressing those pesky feelings.

THE IDEAL SCENARIO

YOU MAKE ME FEEL LIKE A TERRIBLE PERSON FOR NOT GOING TO CHURCH. I KNOW YOU DON'T AGREE WITH ME, BUT SOMETIMES I FEEL LIKE YOU DON'T RESPECT ME EITHER.

I'M SORRY FOR MAKING YOU FEEL THAT WAY, TRULY. WE'RE NEVER GOING TO SEE EYE TO EYE ON THIS, BUT OF COURSE I RESPECT YOU. AND YOUR BELIEFS.

THE NOT-SO-IDEAL SCENARIO
PART 1

Sometimes those confrontations will reveal that the relationship is harboring more negative feelings than you're willing to put up with. And that's good to know too.

For everyday declines, start with an apology + no + end on a positive note.

You can justify a rejection with a good reason and soften it with a request for understanding . . .

If your urge to please is irresistible, try suggesting something that you do feel comfortable with.

Good friends = extra niceness.

A considerate counteroffer meets your needs and theirs.

Not-quite-friends may require some quick thinking—keep your offers neutral.

NOT COMFORTABLE ENOUGH TO RECOMMEND HIM

HEY! LONG TIME NO SPEAK! I'M IN THE MARKET FOR A JOB AND SAW YOUR COMPANY'S HIRING. WOULD YOU MIND RECOMMENDING ME?

HEY!! SEND ME YOUR RESUME! I'D BE HAPPY TO PASS IT ALONG AND MAKE SURE IT GETS SEEN BY THE RIGHT PERSON. THAT'S HALF THE BATTLE OVER HERE :)

THANKS. I'D REALLY APPRECIATE THAT.

SENDING HIS RESUME TO THE HIRING MANAGER (WITH ALL THE APPROPRIATE CAVEATS) IS STILL HELPFUL, WITHOUT TYING YOUR REPUTATION TO SOMEONE YOU'RE NOT COMFORTABLE BEING TIED TO.

No matter where someone falls on the friend spectrum, if they ask you for something and you have a personal policy, lean into it. You're allowed to have "your thing." The more people know about it, the less likely they will be to ask.

It is possible to say no to hosting without being inhospitable—
but you have to be ready. Here are some excuses to practice.

I'M SORRY, BUT BETWEEN WORK AND SOME PERSONAL STUFF, THIS JUST ISN'T A GOOD TIME.

OR

I'M SORRY, BUT MY DOG IS REALLY UNPREDICTABLE WITH STRANGERS!

OR

HEY, STRANGER! I'LL BE IN YOUR NECK OF THE WOODS NEXT WEEK!! DO YOU MIND IF I STAY WITH YOU FOR A FEW DAYS?

I'M SORRY, BUT WE JUST DON'T HAVE THE ROOM.

AND
(OPTIONAL)

I'D LOVE TO SEE YOU WHILE YOU'RE HERE, THOUGH! LET ME KNOW WHEN IS BEST FOR YOU AND I'LL MAKE IT WORK.

If you want to say no, try suggesting a more appropriate substitute.

Postponement is another good tactic; it's okay to buy yourself some time.

When you *are* open to a one-time-only yes, make sure to set those expectations on the front end.

If you don't, things you've agreed to in the past can come back to haunt you. Awkward as it may be, make your new boundaries clear.

Unfortunately, some nos are just hard to soften. Breathe it out and don't cave. A few moments of discomfort are better than doing something you know you can't afford—financially or emotionally.

Sometimes you might have to keep apologizing—but do not back down from your no.

If you sit with the discomfort, it'll pass eventually.

What about those moments when you just . . . can't?
Pro Tip: The Hold-Over Message. A temporary measure, but it
gives you breathing room to come up with something better.

An apology + vulnerability + request for understanding
= an unassailable no!

Energy drainers are dangerous creatures, and the best approach is
to get away from them fast—be ready to announce your getaway.

Watch out for the foregone conclusion attack—a kind of gaslighting that takes your agreement for granted. Don't fall for it—you didn't agree, and you can push back.

Beware of those who push boundaries in the name of friendship—remind them that friendship means sometimes saying no.

It's not just friends who will test your no muscle. Authority figures often have knowledge that you don't, but that doesn't mean they know exactly what's best for you. Honor your instincts, voice your concerns, and resist anything that makes you uncomfortable.

There are people out there who are literally trained to overcome your ability to say no, so you have to train too.

Low-stakes encounters make for good practice runs.

No matter how you slice it, a people pleaser's propensity to prioritize others' feelings above their own can be overwhelming. But, the more you can redirect those inclinations and find ways to turn that compassion inward, the stronger your no muscle will become.

A quick pause can help you get through the initial panic without blurting out an unnecessary yes. Bonus: it makes you seem thoughtful while you figure out how to resist the overload.

A longer pause is helpful when there's a lot at stake.

Or in situations where you're pretty sure this should not be your responsibility—especially if you're talking to someone who outranks you.

The purpose of the pause is to give you time to figure out whether a no is, in fact, the best course of action, or if a yes might be the better route, all things considered.

"HOW TO KNOW WHEN TO SAY NO" RECIPE
CORPORATE STYLE

INGREDIENTS
- IS THIS A REASONABLE REQUEST?
- DOES IT FALL WITHIN YOUR RESPONSIBILITIES?
- HOW WILL IT AFFECT YOUR OTHER RESPONSIBILITIES?
- HOW WILL YOU BE COMPENSATED, FINANCIALLY OR OTHERWISE?
- HOW WILL YOU FEEL AFTER HAVING DONE IT? ("ACCOMPLISHED" OR "TAKEN ADVANTAGE OF" ARE POPULAR CHOICES!)
- WILL DOING IT HELP YOU ACHIEVE A FUTURE GOAL?
- ARE THERE WAYS TO MODIFY THE ASK SO THAT YOU FEEL MORE COMFORTABLE WITH IT?

DIRECTIONS: MIX UP ALL THE ABOVE AND SIT WITH THEM FOR AS LONG AS YOU NEED. FEEL FREE TO TAKE SOME OUT OR ADD MORE IN, DEPENDING ON THE SITUATION. MAKE IT YOUR OWN!

YIELDS: ONE CAREFULLY THOUGHT-OUT DECISION

Note that a corporate no is expressed quite differently.

For less fraught situations, try a quick but polite no with a best wishes topper. If there's a chance you might like to say yes in the future, feel free to let them know.

Mastery: a clear no that also prevents future requests *and* gets you points for being helpful.

Having a full plate is an all-purpose, irrefutable excuse. Keep it ready.

When you start feeling comfortable with the formula, get creative. A multitasking no declines an undesired event while strengthening the work-friend bond with a bit of personal sharing, plus an alternative plan.

Remember that slightly panicked pause? A short break should buy you just enough time to figure out your boundaries and put them out there.

THE JUGGLING ACT
PART 2
THE NOT-SO-IDEAL-SCENARIO

Resist the urge to just give in, and instead try shifting
some of the responsibility back on the person asking.

Pro Tip: Try setting your own terms—in writing. It can help you communicate points that you might not feel comfortable stating in person. (Plus, you can refer back to it if anyone conveniently forgets what they agreed to.)

THE NOT-QUITE-A-PROMOTION
PART 2

To	Ron	
Cc		

Subject: Additional Responsibilities // Follow-up Discussion

Hi Ron,

Thanks again for thinking of me! After reviewing these new responsibilities, I have a few clarifying questions I wanted to lay out in advance of tomorrow's discussion:

- This is a bit of a departure from my current role. Are there any discretionary funds available for professional courses or certifications so that I'm better prepared to tackle these new responsibilities?

- Assuming you're happy with my work, are you open to reevaluating my compensation in three months to be more in line with my new responsibilities? I believe this time frame coincides with finance's annual compensation meeting, but please let me know if I'm mistaken.

Again, I'm very excited about this opportunity and look forward to our discussion!

Best,
Nicole

Whether or not those terms are accepted, however, can give you a lot to think about. Just remember: you have options either way.

THE NOT-QUITE-A-PROMOTION
PART 3

And for those requests that, for whatever reason, get under your skin, the pause is especially important. It gives you time to tone down the snark and come up with a carefully crafted no.

CORPORATE CHAOS
PART 2

TONED DOWN A BIT FROM YESTERDAY'S MORE POINTED "REGARDING YOUR QUESTIONABLY SEXIST REQUEST"

File Message Insert Options Format Text Review Help

Arial | 11 | **B** *I* U

To Frank

Cc

Send

Subject Holiday Event Follow-Up

Hi Frank,

I hope all is well! Following up on yesterday's discussion, given my current role in the company, I don't think I would be best suited to plan this year's holiday event. I do know that our event manager, Kyle, did a great job with last year's holiday event, so it might be worth reaching out to him.

Thanks!
Nicole

THROWING SOMEONE ELSE UNDER THE BUS IS NEVER ADVISED, BUT CLARIFYING ROLES FOR SOMEONE WHO MIGHT NOT UNDERSTAND WHAT THEY ENTAIL, OR REFERENCING PAST WORK IS PERFECTLY ACCEPTABLE.

The true promotion for the people pleaser comes when you can confidently give the word "no" its proper seat at the table.

Regardless of where you find yourself, the word *no* is critical in making sure you get where you need to go—and more importantly, to helping you avoid all the places you don't.

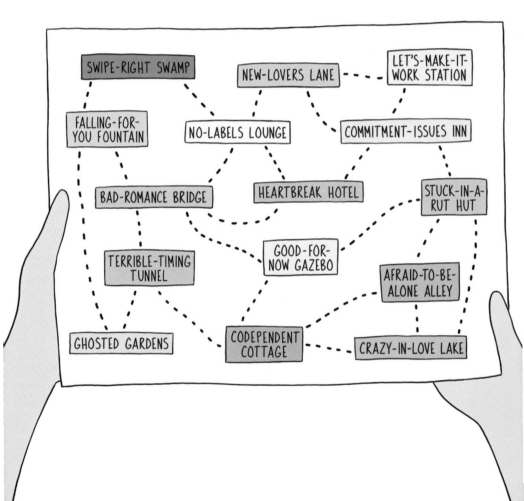

Whether you're flirting, dating, or falling in love (or out of love), no will need to be said, and it won't always be easy.

Being candid can be hard when egos are fragile and situations are fraught, so the finesse you've been developing is going to be key. It helps to have a range of ready-to-use phrases handy.

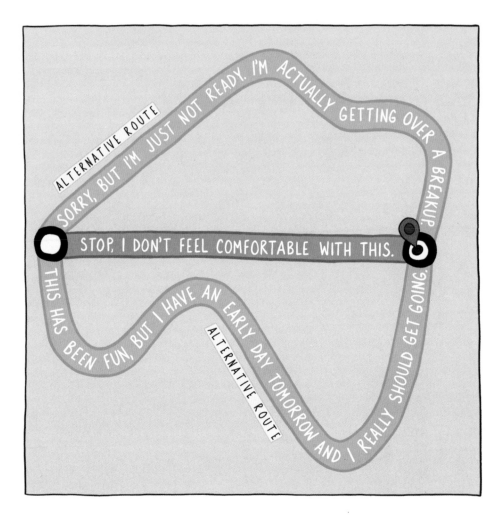

You can still be mindful of feelings, while remaining firm.

Everyone loves playing Cupid, but don't let other people's good intentions undermine your resolve.

As soon as you know someone's not right for you,
bring out your nicest no.

Misunderstandings are inevitable.

HAD A 45-SECOND POLITE BUT ALTOGETHER UNREMARKABLE CONVERSATION ABOUT THE WEATHER

IF NECESSARY

YOU CAN'T CONTROL HOW OTHER PEOPLE REACT TO YOUR BOUNDARIES, SO IF THE SITUATION BECOMES UNSAFE, YOUR PRIORITY SHOULD BE TO GET OUT.

There will be situations where you find yourself taken aback.

Remarkably, people still try this. No need for you to be polite.

The line between friendship and romance can get blurry. If you're crystal clear on where you stand, kind but firm usually works.

No matter where you are in the dating game, you'll have to deal with the question of consent. There is only one indisputable rule you have to remember: You are in charge of your game. You decide what you want.

Develop a mental playbook—a game plan for every situation.
Practice each play so you're comfortable when you need to use it.

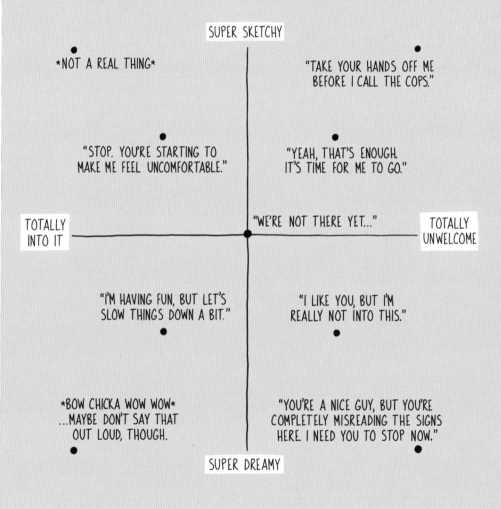

DIFFERENT WAYS TO CALL IT...

SUPER SKETCHY

NOT A REAL THING

"TAKE YOUR HANDS OFF ME
BEFORE I CALL THE COPS."

"STOP. YOU'RE STARTING TO
MAKE ME FEEL UNCOMFORTABLE."

"YEAH, THAT'S ENOUGH.
IT'S TIME FOR ME TO GO."

TOTALLY
INTO IT

"WE'RE NOT THERE YET..."

TOTALLY
UNWELCOME

"I'M HAVING FUN, BUT LET'S
SLOW THINGS DOWN A BIT."

"I LIKE YOU, BUT I'M
REALLY NOT INTO THIS."

BOW CHICKA WOW WOW
...MAYBE DON'T SAY THAT
OUT LOUD, THOUGH.

"YOU'RE A NICE GUY, BUT YOU'RE
COMPLETELY MISREADING THE SIGNS
HERE. I NEED YOU TO STOP NOW."

SUPER DREAMY

When you finally find someone you want to be with, you'll still need to keep your no muscle in shape. Boundaries make for a healthy relationship, and not communicating them can wreak havoc.

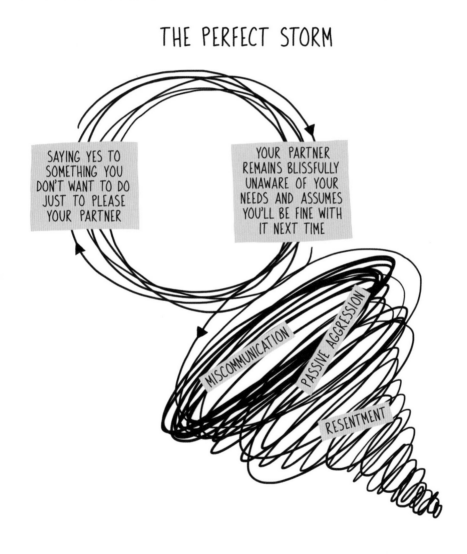

THE PERFECT STORM

SAYING YES TO SOMETHING YOU DON'T WANT TO DO JUST TO PLEASE YOUR PARTNER

YOUR PARTNER REMAINS BLISSFULLY UNAWARE OF YOUR NEEDS AND ASSUMES YOU'LL BE FINE WITH IT NEXT TIME

MISCOMMUNICATION

PASSIVE AGGRESSION

RESENTMENT

Getting good at saying no to seemingly minor things . . .

...BULLET DODGED

The way the little nos of a relationship are received will go a long way in making you feel more confident in moving forward, knowing the big nos will be respected down the line.

All healthy relationships are a balancing act.

But, just because a relationship is great, doesn't necessarily mean it's meant to last forever. That's when a strong no muscle steps up.

And with all that practice saying no . . .
you'll know when to say yes.

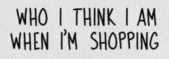

WHO I THINK I AM
WHEN I'M SHOPPING

Remember to keep in mind what's best for future you, not just right-now you.

In the long run, telling yourself no can actually be more rewarding than the temporary high of yes.

Sometimes you just have to learn the hard way.

If pausing is your secret weapon when saying no to others, then logic is your secret weapon when saying no to yourself. Some of our most toxic thoughts are completely irrational.

Comparing ourselves to others is another trap that's easy to fall into.

THE RANDOM STRANGER'S INSTAGRAM STORY

Illogical to the point of absurdity: comparing ourselves to imaginary ideals.

Perfection is another trap, unrealistic and sometimes even harmful.

ACTUAL PICTURE OF MY VERY FIRST
INSTAGRAM POST THAT, YEARS
LATER, LED TO THIS BOOK DEAL

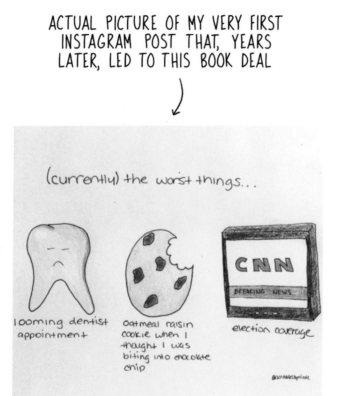

(currently) the worst things...

looming dentist
appointment

oatmeal raisin
cookie when I
thought I was
biting into chocolate
chip

election coverage

@scribblesbynicole

IF I HAD WAITED UNTIL I KNEW HOW
TO DRAW, OR KNEW EXACTLY WHAT I
WANTED TO SAY, I'D STILL BE WAITING

Say no to your urge to put on a perfect front.

It's okay for things to not be okay.

If self-deprecation is your go-to, practice not giving in to it.

Embracing compliments is far more rewarding for everyone.

Your inner critic will probably always be there, but don't let her get the last word.

Show yourself the kindness you automatically afford to everyone else.

And remember, when things get *really* tough, you don't have to fight alone.

Missteps are inevitable—that's how you find your footing.

FLEXING YOUR NO MUSCLE

Remember, no matter how tentatively you started out . . .

I don't think I can go next week

I'm not sure I can help right now.

I'm sorry, but I don't think I can do that.

with a little finesse, a bit of confidence, and enough practice, you'll get the hang of it.

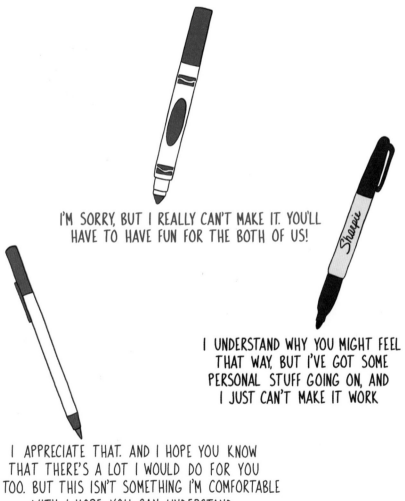

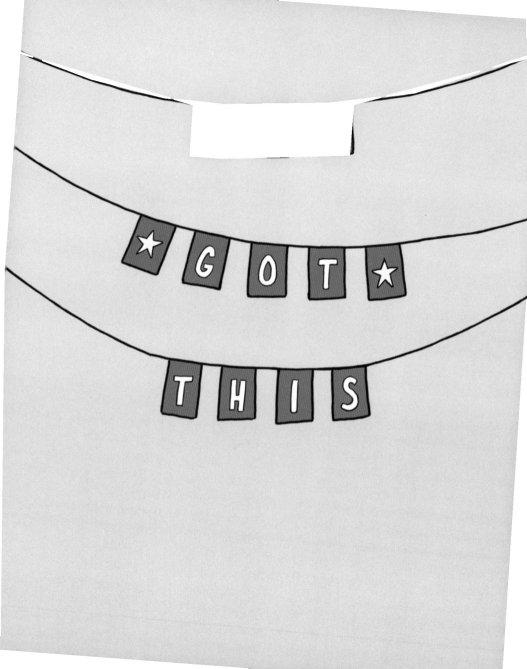

First and foremost, I want to thank Mario, for supporting my every whim, for being in my corner every step of the way, and for dealing with the boring stuff so I don't have to. There's no one else I'd rather go through this life with. To my mom, whose little talks somehow manage to make me feel like the smartest, funniest, most capable woman in the world (which is no easy feat, for obvious reasons). To my incredible friends–the most loyal, least judgmental, genuinely best people I could possibly imagine. I'd be lost without you guys. To Nino, whose kindness, generosity, and cooking is as inspiring as it is eternally appreciated. To Mario's family, for the endless love, support, and food you've given me over the years. To everyone on Instagram who has ever supported my work; without your encouragement, I would have never had the confidence to make this happen. And finally, to my publisher Sharyn and her wonderful team. Everyone on this list is great and all, but without you, this book literally would not have happened. I'm forever grateful.

Cue the music

Printed in China

SPRUCE BOOKS with colophon is a registered trademark of Penguin Random House LLC

25 24 23 22   9 8 7 6 5 4 3 2 1

Editor: Sharyn Rosart
Production editor: Peggy Gannon
Designer: Alicia Terry

ISBN: 978-1-63217-443-7

Spruce Books, a Sasquatch Books Imprint
1325 Fourth Avenue, Suite 1025
Seattle, WA 98101

SasquatchBooks.com

MIX
Paper | Supporting responsible forestry
FSC® C008047
FSC
www.fsc.org

ABOUT THE AUTHOR

Nicole Monente shares her musings at @scribblesbynicole, where she's captured the hearts and minds of a significant following with her clever, introspective, and ultra-relatable drawings. Nicole approaches heavy topics with humor, lightheartedness, and insight. When she's not doodling, Nicole can be found laughing, crying, or desperately looking for her phone to jot down her next idea before she forgets it. Nicole lives and draws in Bergen County, New Jersey.